A day in the life of
Zoe the vet

Monica Hughes

Heinemann
LIBRARY

Little Nippers

www.heinemann.co.uk/library
Visit our website to find out more information about **Heinemann Library** books.

To order:
☎ Phone 44 (0) 1865 888066
▤ Send a fax to 44 (0) 1865 314091
▯ Visit the Heinemann Bookshop at www.heinemann.co.uk/library to browse our catalogue and order online.

First published in Great Britain by Heinemann Library, Halley Court, Jordan Hill, Oxford OX2 8EJ, part of Harcourt Education.
Heinemann is a registered trademark of Harcourt Education Ltd.

Editorial: Jilly Attwood and Claire Throp
Design: Jo Hinton-Malivoire and bigtop, Bicester, UK
Models made by: Jo Brooker
Picture Research: Catherine Bevan
Production: Lorraine Warner

Originated by Dot Gradations
Printed and bound in China by South China Printing Company

ISBN 0 431 16524 6 (hardback)
06 05 04 03 02
10 9 8 7 6 5 4 3 2 1

ISBN 0 431 16529 7 (paperback)
06 05 04 03 02
10 9 8 7 6 5 4 3 2 1

British Library Cataloguing in Publication Data
Hughes, Monica
    A day in the life of a vet
    636.089
A full catalogue record for this book is available from the British Library.

Acknowledgements
The publishers would like to thank the following for permission to reproduce photographs:
All photos by Tudor Photography.

Cover photograph reproduced with permission of Tudor Photography.

Special thanks to Clive Madeiros, Zoe Kirk and all the staff at West Bar Veterinary Surgery, Banbury.

The publishers would like to thank Annie Davy for her assistance in the preparation of this book.

Every effort has been made to contact copyright holders of any material reproduced in this book. Any omissions will be rectified in subsequent printings if notice is given to the publishers.

Contents

Meet Zoe the vet 4

Before work 6

The day starts 8

The first patient 10

More patients 12

Another patient 14

It's time for lunch! 16

The operating theatre 18

After the operation 20

The day ends 22

Index 24

Meet Zoe the vet

Zoe

Bonzo

Have you ever taken an animal to see a vet?

Then Zoe sets off for work.

The day starts

Zoe changes into her uniform at work.

Then she checks the animals who had to stay overnight.

The first patient

Cameron has brought his cat to see the vet for a check-up.

miaow

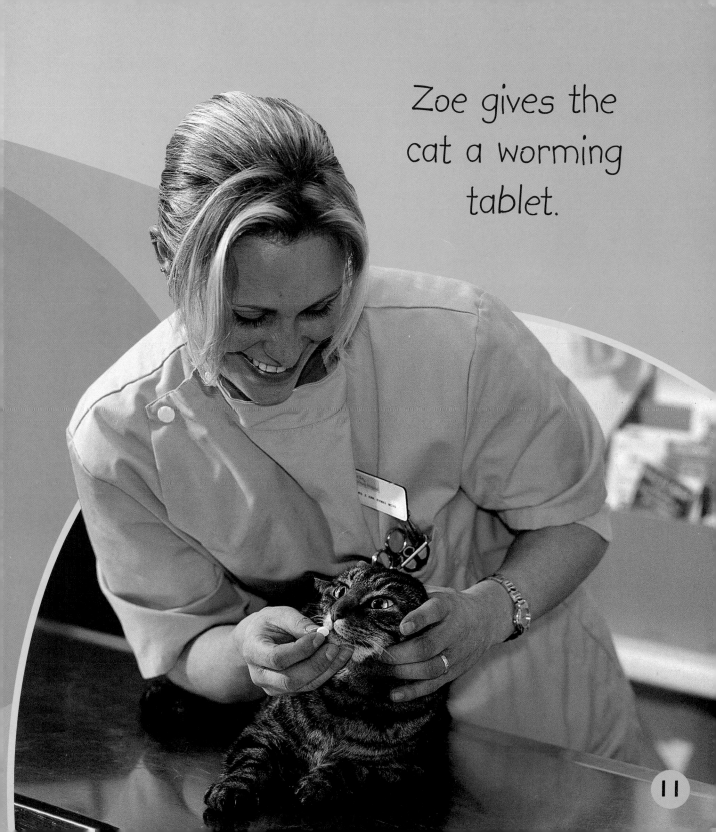

Zoe gives the cat a worming tablet.

11

More patients

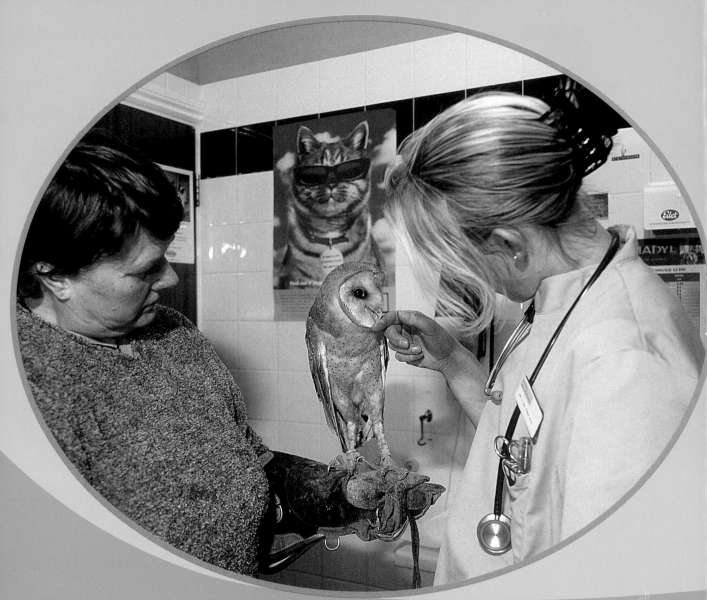

This rescued owl has come
to have its beak clipped.

Zoe examines a dog with a bad heart.

Another patient

A rabbit has to have its claws clipped because they are too long.

clip

clip

clip

15

It's time for lunch!

Yum!

16

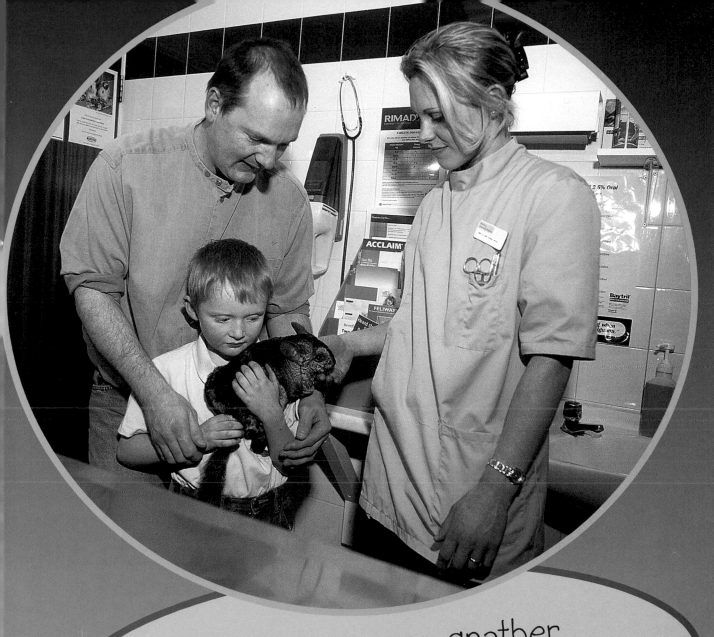

After lunch Zoe sees another patient. This time it is a chinchilla.

The operating theatre

Zoe 'scrubs up' and changes to get ready for the operation.

splish

splash

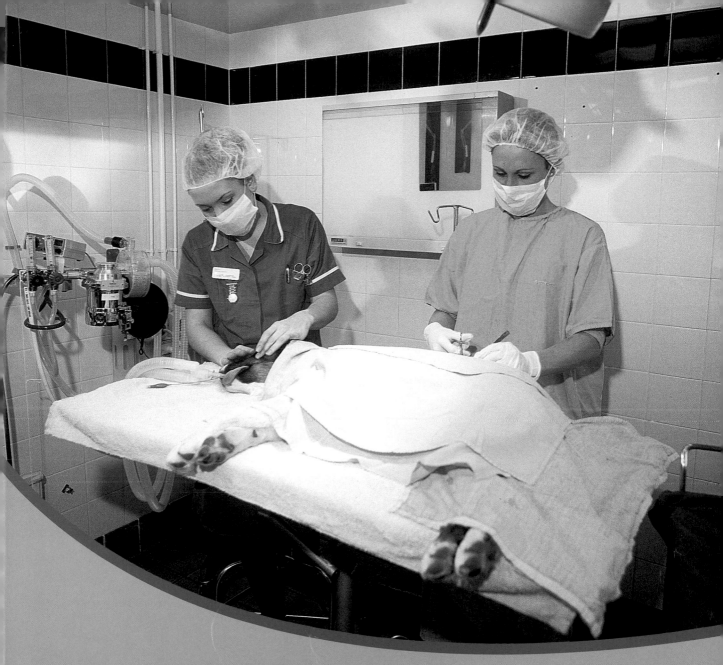

Don't worry, the patient doesn't feel anything during the operation.

After the operation

Zoe checks the patient after the operation.

The dog is OK.

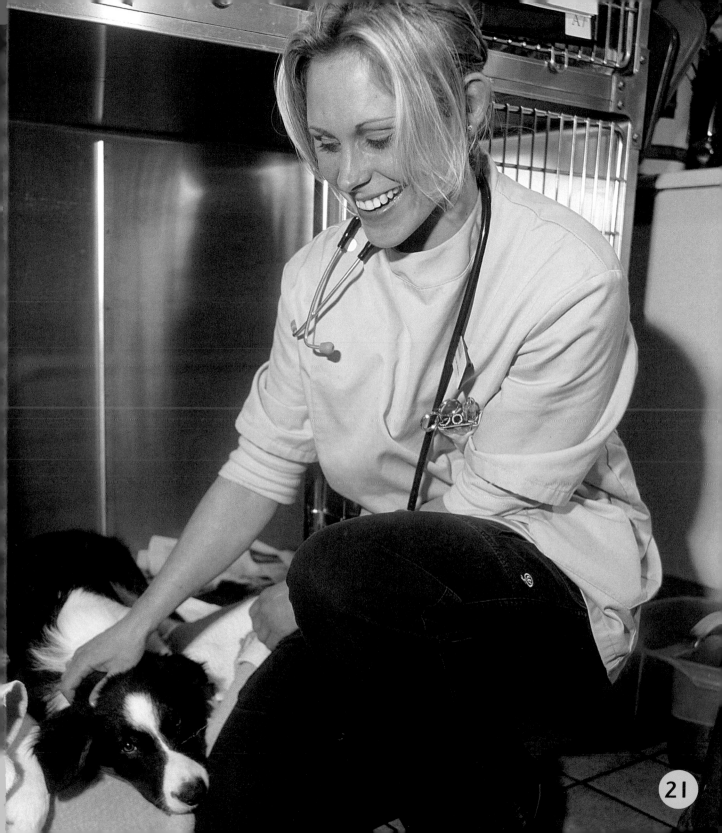

The day ends

After work Zoe likes to relax.

She takes her phone to bed.

Zoe might get a call in the night if any of the animals need her help.

Index

bedtime 23

cat 10, 11

chinchilla 17

dog 6, 13, 20

operation 18, 19

owl 12

rabbit 14

uniform 9

The end

Notes for adults

This series supports the young child's exploration of their learning environment and their knowledge and understanding of their world. The following Early Learning Goals are relevant to the series:
• Respond to significant experiences, showing a range of feelings when appropriate.
• Find out about events that they observe.
• Ask questions about why things happen and how things work.
• Find out about and identify the uses of everyday technology to support their learning.

The series shows the different jobs four professionals do and provides opportunities to compare and contrast them. The books show that like everyone else, including young children, they get up in the morning, go to bed at night, break for meals, and have families, pets and a life outside their work.

The books will help the child to extend their vocabulary, as they will hear new words. Some of the words that may be new to them in **A Day in the Life of a Vet** are patient, 'check-up', worming, beak, clipped, examine, claws, chinchilla, operation and 'scrubs up'. Since words are used in context in the book this should enable the young child to gradually incorporate them into their own vocabulary.

The following additional information may be of interest:
During an operation a nurse assists the vet. Both the vet and the nurse wear protective clothing. The animal is given an anaesthetic and the nurse checks its breathing during the operation. The animal is an in-patient until it has recovered from the operation.

Follow-up activities

The child could role play situations in a vet's surgery. Areas could be set up to create a consulting room, operating theatre and cages for in-patients. The child could also record what they have found out by drawing, painting or tape recording their experiences.

24